Motherhood
a celebration

BY LENORE SKOMAL

Kennebunkport, Maine

To the person I love most in the world—my son.
This one's for you, Nate.

Motherhood: A Celebration

13 Digit ISBN: 978-1-933662-60-2
10 Digit ISBN: 1-933662-60-3

This book may be ordered by mail from the publisher. Please include $4.50 for postage and handling.
Please support your local bookseller first!

Books published by Cider Mill Press Book Publishers are available at special discounts for bulk purchases in the United States by corporations, institutions, and other organizations. For more information, please contact the publisher.

Cider Mill Press Book Publishers
"Where good books are ready for press"
12 Port Farm Road
Kennebunkport, Maine 04046

Visit us on the web!
www.cidermillpress.com

Design by Alicia Freile
Typography: Bellevue, Bulmer, Futura, New Baskerville, Optima
All illustrations courtesy of Photodisc.
Printed in China

1 2 3 4 5 6 7 8 9 0
First Edition

CONTENTS

Chapter One: *A Mother Is Born*

7

Chapter Two: *The Greatest Love of All*

19

Chapter Three: *The Deep Roots of Nurturing*

39

Chapter Four: *A Legacy of Love*

49

Chapter Five: *The Art of Mothering: Words and Wisdom*

57

A Mother
Is Born

*I never thought that you should be rewarded
for the greatest privilege of life.*

May Roper Coker, on being chosen Mother of the Year

*T*he journey of motherhood begins with a tiny wail. And it takes your breath away. It's the first sound that marks the unforgettable moment, which will be forever etched on your soul and secreted away in your heart where you can touch and relive it at any time. It's the primal cry—the first sound that your newborn makes in this world. It's the first utterance that decries a new independence. For this life was once a part of you, nurtured deep inside your womb. And now, miraculously, this new creature is in your arms, outside of the warmth and protection of your natural body.

That first cry on this earth heralds the arrival of a new life, announcing this miracle of nature, calling out, "Yes, yes, I am here." That little cry is the first impact that this new soul makes on this planet. Your baby is now a part of the greater whole. He or she is an integral addition to what we call humanity and the family of man. And that addition is charged to you, to love and nurture with a newly discovered but abundant source of love.

It's the tiniest of cries but what an impact that smallest of vibrations has. It alone has the power to awaken a love so deep and abiding, so overpowering, that it shocks your system. While you had loved before, you have never loved like this. In that very instant, your "self" dissolves, and all that remains important is your child. You now know what it means to love someone with such wild abandon that you are willing and eager to do anything to ensure his or her safety. This is your first taste of unconditional love. It remains one of the greatest gifts that you are given during the journey of motherhood. The love of and for your child supercedes any other love in life.

When it is all said and done, the transformation from one to two creates not only a new child, but a new mother as well.

In the sheltered simplicity of the first days after a baby is born, one sees again the magical closed circle, the miraculous sense of two people existing only for each other.

Anne Morrow Lindbergh, Aviator

The process of birthing a child teaches you one of the most fundamental of life lessons—namely, that you are, at your very core, part of something much greater than the sum total of yourself. This lesson may not be new. It may have been something that you intellectually understood, or perhaps were taught in your respective faith. But the actual physical act of laboring your child into the world makes that lesson part and parcel of your life experience. It creates a lasting impression. It is the ability to bring another life force into existence, to be the vessel by which another being takes shape, to co-create with nature and ultimately continue the circle of life. Grant it, you have but a small hand in creating this miracle. But it is your miracle, one that will continue to mesmerize, consume, inspire, and adore you for the rest of your mortal life. A baby. Your baby.

The beauty and wonder of your motherhood starts with carrying that life deep within you. You cry over the heartbeat, suffer with heartburn, panic over lack of movement, and watch with horror and amazement as your body deforms and stretches to inhuman proportions—all the while never quite truly grasping what is happening inside of you. Without being able to see inside your body, it's very difficult to fully understand that there is a baby in there—another individual. Do you every truly understand that for this brief while, this short nine months of gestation, you are completely and utterly one being? This new life is reliant on your body for sustenance and nurturing, growth and development—completely dependant on you, wholly and solely. It will be the last time in your child's life when this is true. From the moment of your child's birth, raising his or her life is now a process of letting go.

The pain of childbirth is one with great purpose. It teaches a poignant lesson—one that will serve you throughout your life: We have no real control in this world, just the perception of such. In order to allow your baby to be born, the ultimate control belongs to neither your body nor the baby. It's taken over by something so much larger than that. The Hopi elders teach that birth is like being in the midst of a rushing river. Clinging to the banks or a large rock won't help. Fighting the current will be futile and only make things harder. Let go, they say, and let the river carry you. In the transitional moments of childbirth, you feel that life force, driving through you, bringing your baby to life. It is a humbling experience.

Giving birth is one of those rare moments that allows you the briefest touch with the thundering force of the universe, which has a tempo and rhythm all its own. Birth grants you the greatest of gifts—learning how to work with, not against this natural force. It is an awe-inspiring act of complete selflessness. You are holding hands with God to create.

Discovering that with every child, your heart grows bigger and strong, that there is no limit to how much or how many people you can love, even though at times you feel as though you could burst. You don't. You just love even more.

Yasmin Le Bon, Fashion Model

Birth opens the new door to motherhood, a door that leads to a lifetime of incredible epiphanies, loving moments, breathtaking joy, as well as internal struggles. It's a continual game of push-me-pull-you. The line that you have to walk teeters on your natural desire to cling, protect, and keep your child close. But you know that you have to eventually let out enough rope to let your child move away. With every stage and each step, you have a choice of whether or not to grow, too.

Motherhood gives you the soil to grow into your better self. It gives you the foundation and the multiple opportunities that dare you to dig deeper in order to spirit yourself higher to develop into the best that you can be. It keeps teaching and instructing. It challenges you to stretch your small life in a much larger net that breathes and releases and never restrains but always loves. It throws down the gauntlet, challenging you to continually refine and polish your character and mature in your concept of love.

When your child was born, love stopped being a centralized concept. Rather than being me-centered, it becomes other-centered, a light beam shooting from the heart, directed and focused on your child. The great love for your child naturally pushes you to strive to be the best mother that you can be.

Your love continues to challenge you each step along the way. First you must understand the boundary between you and your child. Happily, you don't have to do a thing to define that boundary. Nature and your baby take care of that on their own. The defining process begins with your baby's first attempt to hold onto something and then leads to his or her first baby step. Your baby then walks away from all that is familiar into the unfamiliar.

If love is the first lesson, then trust in self is the second that your love teaches. Your love for your child is not selfish; it is worldly. You yearn for the best for your child. You know that a young heart raised with nonjudgmental, selfless love and nurturing will grow into a brave heart, able and willing to embrace the world and treat it with kindness. Perhaps the greatest love of all is a mother's love, because therein lies the capacity to create a generation of sensitive, broad-minded souls who do not belong to their mothers, but to the world.

Maud Tousey Fangel

> *Children are the hands by which*
> *we take hold of heaven.*

Henry Ward Beecher, Clergyman

Your child's birth is a deeply personal, empowering moment that will stay with you the rest of your life—an event unsurpassed by any other. It has the power to buoy you during the tough times when despair is threatening to halt you in your track and stymie you in your personal development. It can inspire you to believe that anything is possible. After all, if you can create a child, a human being where nothing before existed, why are you limiting yourself? The universe is expansive and lies within each one of us. The memory of childbirth also allows you never to feel alone, for you truly are not. Birthing a child ties you eternally to all that is good and right and just in your universe. You are forever connected to it and to the rest of us. Tapping into that experience is your right as a mother, and it can be your salvation.

Every baby is your baby. No child can go without, once you have experienced unconditional motherly love. The soul of each and every baby is the soul of your baby. Once you open the door to mothering your child, you also mother the world. Babies confirm your eternal nature and your promise of hope. Think of the inherent power in just the act of holding a baby? The smell of the top of the baby's head has instant healing powers. It's vulnerability, innocence, angelic virtue, and love all wrapped in one tiny body. There is not a human spirit alive that doesn't respond immediately to a baby—awakening feelings of protectiveness, awe, and sweetness in even the hardest of hearts. That is the power of a baby.

Yes, birthing your baby does something to your soul. It transforms it on many levels. The first transformation happens almost immediately—the unconditional, all-encompassing love coupled with a desperate sense of protectiveness, overwhelming desire to nurture, and abiding, yet fierce, loyalty to your tiny human. That initial change marks the beginning of the metamorphosis which will become the joy of mothering, a glorious, mysterious journey that began with that first, tiny wail.

The
Greatest Love
of All

A baby is God's opinion that
the world should go on.

Carl Sandburg, Poet

*T*ransformation is a funny thing. It twists the perception on your life so that nothing looks quite the same anymore. Your maternal instinct is born with your new baby; many manifest long before that. There is no such thing as sacrifice when it comes to your child—just prioritizing.

But much of the change that unfolds after the door to motherhood is opened is not heralded by the same awe-inspiring miracle experienced through birth. Rather, the transformation that you undergo is subtly woven into the tapestry of your life, intricately threaded as your child grows and matures. It's a road graced with enough ups and downs to forge an iron-bond between the two of you. There is now a secret, steely cord, connecting yet invisible, that ties you together forever. This bond cannot be changed by anyone, except the two of you.

It was my mother who gave me my voice. She did this, I know now, by clearing a space where my words could fall, grow, then find their way to others.

Paula Giddings, Writer

Babyhood goes by so fast. Your child's amazing accomplishments and changes multiply each day. While enthralling, it can also be overwhelming. For becoming a mother has also ushered in a continual sense of anxiety. You spend most of your days worrying. And that will never change. First you hover over your child, and then you show concern over the tiniest things. You dissect every aspect of your child's development, worried that something might not be on schedule, not quite right. At every turn, you question yourself. Second guessing becomes second nature. *Am I doing this right?*

This is a magical time of fairy dust dances, tales of Santa and guardian angels, and things that go bump in the night. The power of this magic is so great that even you want to believe. This time of early childhood and wonder is a gift of memories. And, oh, the

memories you will collect—albums of them, tucked away in your heart, to relish forever. You'll be able to smell that bald little head, recall the feel of your baby's chubby thighs, and remember how your heart soared every time you looked into those saucer eyes staring at you in wide-eyed adoration. It's an amazing time and perhaps the one meant to sustain you during the times to come when your patience and good nature are tested, and you're left pondering whatever happened to that cute, little cherub.

Furnish an example, stop preaching, stop shielding, don't prevent self-reliance and initiative, allow your children to develop along their own lines.

Eleanor Roosevelt, U.S. First Lady

With the coming years, your worries change and shift, as do you. As growth and change march across your world, you continue to worry about every aspect of it. The smallest thing could be a cause for alarm. When your child is not with you, you worry even more. Without your vigilant eye, who knows what could happen. Who could possibly care for your little one like you?

This is the natural path of mothers everywhere. Worry and concern come part and parcel with the gift of creating and raising a child. Accepting it for what it is—an outcropping of overwhelming love—is the key to honoring it. Letting it get the best of you is quite the opposite.

While the concern never ever goes away completely, it does change. But you are the one who has to change it. Motherhood starts with learning to trust "self." Then it slowly shifts to trusting your child. You believe in him or her. You honor your child as an individual. This respect and trust fuels hope, which helps temper your worry. Only then, can you understand that, yes, it will all be fine. Life will unfold in the manner in which it is supposed to. Yes, there will be ups and downs, but part of the growing process is being able to allow and accept that for your child and for yourself.

While worry is natural, it's the ability to keep fear at bay and worry in check that allows the greater gifts to flow through. And the blessings are many. There is only one you; only one mother to your child. Whether you both know it or not, you are unique to each other, more than any two people in the world. It's stark honesty that is sometimes more than can be born by the average soul. It's overwhelming. Being able to feel that love in all its intensity is the joy of mothering. Don't allow worry to block that.

While the hugs may diminish over time, the trust and responsibility that goes along with them doesn't. It just changes. It's the same child who once held on for dear life in the middle of the night. It's the same child that gripped your hand until it hurt, when walking into a roomful of strangers. It's the same child who treated you like a heliocentric universe, with you at the center. It's the same person, the same soul—just growing up.

There is always one moment in childhood when the door opens and lets in the future.

Graham Greene, Writer

Growing up means letting go—a little bit at a time. And it's possibly the most challenging aspect of mothering, requiring you to dig deep, plumb the depths of insecurity, develop maturity and wisdom, and overcome the itching desire to pull close and hold tight. If a child stayed a child, there would be something overtly wrong. The cycle of life requires maturity—for both mother and baby.

The greatest part of motherhood is being able to embrace the change before it ever reveals itself. Because before you know it and somehow even under your vigilant lookout, your child does grow up. Knowing that change is a constant in this thing called mothering helps you enjoy the experience to the fullest. You have to live in the moment and love every moment of the journey.

Face it, not all the moments are filled with awe and joy. What mother doesn't long for some relief from hourly feedings, being awoken several times at night, changing endless diapers, calming a screaming child? Who wouldn't like a few minutes to herself, sans the neediness of a child? You wouldn't be human if child-rearing was a simple task, filled with breezy moments and no bumps. It is the rare mother who doesn't get tired, stressed, or cranky. But it is the wise mother who embraces all of it, knowing that this too shall pass. And often times, all too quickly.

Change is a funny thing. It comes like a thief in the night and strikes quickly. And before you know it, that stage in your child's life that seemed never-ending, abruptly ends. And another stage has begun. It's a cycle, and one that is ever-changing. When viewed from the perspective of a lifetime, your child is only a child for a brief period of time. Why miss one bit of it while wasting precious time fretting about the future?

Drink it all in. It's a challenge, but a worthy one, to develop the maturity to see the entire picture, as well as unending maternal compassion for the present. It helps bring perspective to even the most trying of life phases. You may feel stressed out now, but if you deal with this stage poorly or miss it altogether, you may regret it later.

In the long run, all you have are the tools that you develop for yourself and those that you give to your children. The tools that a mother develops and instills in her child will ultimately determine his or her capability in the world.

As a parent you try to maintain a certain amount of control and so you have this tug-of-war. You have to learn when to let go. And that's not easy.

Aretha Franklin, Singer

When to let go and how much is a continual question of motherhood. Quite frankly it starts at birth. Over the next 18 years, you will learn to let go and your child will feel stronger and more confident in risk taking. It's an intuitive process, one relying on a mother's strong understanding of her child, tempered by common sense and her view of life.

It is natural to want to hang on, to continue to worry, and to live solely for your child. While the "want" is natural, doing it is not. A great disservice is done to your child when he or she is forced to walk the fine line of guilt and love, and oft times interchanging the two without distinction. No mother is justified in crippling a child by never allowing independence to come in. It is part of growing up.

Independence comes long before a child is ready to leave home. It comes in the form of developing friendships, socializing with the greater world, developing individual opinion and judgment, bucking authority, and even stepping on the hearts of those most loved. And that can be the hardest.

When your child pushes against you—you, the mother of infinite patience during screaming fits, protector against monsters under the bed, comforter of hurt feelings, once the center of the universe—it is only human to be hurt, and perhaps confused. No one ever said it would be easy to be the whipping post.

Motherhood is a funny thing. It gives you the greatest of gifts—true love. But in return, it requires you to develop a steely strength to insulate you from being eaten by your own worry, to fight to better yourself, to raise your child beyond your own expectation, and then have the grace and maturity to let your child go. Somewhere along the line, your heart runs the awful risk of being torn in two. And you know what? It will. Maybe more than once.

Nothing else ever will make you as happy or as sad, as proud or as tired, for nothing is quite as hard as helping a person develop his own individuality especially while you struggle to keep your own.

Marguerite Kelly and Elia Parsons, Writers

As your child's fight for independence ensues, the closer the two of you are, the scrappier the fight. In a bittersweet way, nothing could be truer in a mother-child relationship. But it is a testimony to the relationship that you have built. For when a child feels completely and utterly loved and comfortable in that love, and has been treated with integrity and support, it would only make sense that honesty is what you'll get in return. Would you want it any other way?

For many times in life, you do hurt the one you love the most, because you can truly be yourself in your rawest form and entrust your ugliness to someone who loves you without judgment—someone like a mother.

While your own strength, boundaries, and even sanity are tested, the battle itself is not about you. It's about independence. It's about a natural pulling away from what it comfortable and known, to what isn't. Never forget that for everything that you are personally going through, all the hits that you are taking and the anguish that you might experience internally—for your child, it's much harder. After all, you have been the adult all these years. He or she is just starting to become one. It takes an enormous amount of courage to be that defiant. Your child is also experiencing a lot of internal conflict. It's difficult to hurt the person you love most, especially the one person who has stood by you, in front of you, and behind you for your entire life.

It's painful. Battles often are. But there is no way around it. Ripping off the biggest part of yourself and expecting it not to hurt is unrealistic. But to keep it attached for the rest of your life, is unnatural and serves no one in the end.

The line is a fine one during this final fight for independence. Both of you deserve respect. In life, every action has an equal and opposite reaction. For every cause, there is an effect. Not necessarily punishment, but always effect. Not being able to draw the distinction between the two gives a child one less tool to use in living life. Not feeling the effects of one's action or having any recourse, is living life in a vacuum.

The truth is that life's expectations should be mirrored each and every day at home. The difference between life in your home and in the outside world is the loving environment you, as a mother, provide. Your home is a safe, experimental ground to translate life's lessons, interpret its injustices, and teach the tools for living a happy and responsible life.

*There are two lasting bequests
we can give our children:
One is roots.
The other is wings.*

Hodding Carter, Jr., Writer

You know it's been coming—from the first day of formal school, the first sleepover, the first best friend, the first goodbye without a kiss, the first dance, the first date, the first day of college, and the first apartment. Life with a child is a series of firsts, which arouse the most confusing and complicated emotions tied to mothering. There is soaring joy, shameless pride, and ecstasy in every first, tempered by fear and worry, which are tough habits to break. And underneath all of that is the tiniest ribbon of sadness as yet another door on childhood closes. *It's all going too fast.* Welcome to the toughest part of mothering.

Snuggles wane all too soon. Hugs become shorter and more hurried. Kisses come and go, and sometimes are brushed off with a thoughtless swipe of the back of a hand. Friends replace family for preferred fun times. The activities multiply; school work piles up and gets harder and beyond your scope to help. It's time for summer jobs, car rides, and parties. And then your child is off to college or is just moving away.

That is perhaps the first time you will have to really say goodbye. College and moving out isn't just a simple task of waving goodbye and calling out niceties to keep in touch. It is the end of a journey that began almost two decades ago. It marks closure to the time in both your lives where your relationship was intricately intertwined. Your roles have now abruptly and completely changed. You no longer are responsible for this person in the way in which you once were. And this adult-child is now at every level, independent. There is only so much control that you can exert once the car drives away for the first and final time.

Sure, the bedroom will stand as a shrine to times gone by. The reluctance to remove trophies, hair ribbons, and dated posters is natural. Clinging to something that once was is commonplace. It happens with any major life change. However always looking back at what was, isn't the best perspective. It keeps you from looking at what is. And that is so much more rewarding.

Now that your child is gone, what have you got? An independent adult. A supportive, maturing relationship. An enormous heart filled with so many priceless memories. A lifetime of more of the same. This was once the small baby in your arms. So many things could have gone wrong. So many things may have. But isn't that the mystery of life?

The continual question about the ups and downs, of how it all unfolds? Is it predestined, is it all scripted in the end? Or is it really a crap shoot?

Be secure in the fact that all things happen for a reason. And your constant nurturing, continual worry, testing of your patience, all those sleepless nights, and each and every unsung and unknown sacrifice—it's all worth it. Make no mistake, it is you who have scripted this. In all those moments when you doubted yourself, thought you couldn't do it, you never gave up. You believed when belief was a vague and faraway concept. You loved when others said you shouldn't. You gave when you had nothing to give.

You did what you needed to do.

What a ride it's been!

And just think. It all began with that tiny wail.

The Deep Roots *of* Nurturing

Every mother is like Moses.
She does not enter the promised land.
She prepares a world she will not see.

Pope John Paul VI

*P*agan religions have exalted the image of the goddess mother long before Christianity, stemming back to the concept of an Earth Mother or Mother Goddess or Great Goddess, which derives primarily from the Greeks. In the *Theogony*, written in the early 7th century B.C.E., the poet Hesiod named the "deep-breasted" Earth Gaea, "a firm seat of all things for ever," who, after emerging out of Chaos, brought forth the sky, mountains, the sea, and, after having lain with Ouranus, a number of non-cosmological Titans. There was also a sanctuary of Earth the Nursing-Mother near the entrance to the Acropolis in Athens. Greeks also honored Rhea, the Mother of the Gods, by bringing honey cakes and flowers during an annual spring festival. The Romans adopted their own mythology about a mother goddess, worshiping her as Tellus, or *Terra Mater,* also called the Great Mother or Earth Mother.

Images of mothers possess the qualities of birth, nurturing, and protecting. Mothers are shown as providers of all-encompassing, unconditional love. Suckling babies are often depicted with mother goddesses, as are icons of Mary, the mother of Jesus, and Eve, the mother of mankind.

Great mothers of history, whether fictional, mythological or real, are revered for selfless love, protection of humanity and child, dedication, and undying loyalty.

Becoming a mother makes you the mother of all children. From now on each wounded, abandoned, frightened child is yours. You live in the suffering mothers of every race and creed and weep with them. You long to comfort all who are desolate.

Charlotte Gray, Writer

Honoring mothers goes back to the Greeks, but early Christians carried on the celebration by creating a festival on the fourth Sunday of Lent in honor of the Virgin Mary. Later, in England, an ecclesiastical order expanded the holiday to include all mothers, and decreed it as Mothering Sunday. Servants would have the day off and were encouraged to return home and spend the day with their mothers. When the first English colonists settled in America the tradition stopped. It wasn't until 1872, when Julia Ward Howe (1819–1910), the author of the lyrics to "The Battle Hymn of the Republic," established a day for mothers honoring peace.

But it was Anna Jarvis who is considered the mother of Mother's Day. When Anna Jarvis set about to have a day commemorating all mothers in the early 1900s, she did so as a tribute to her own mother, Ann Jarvis, a defining force in her life. Her mother was a formidable woman, birthing 11 children of which only four reached adulthood. A civic organizer, she worked to combat poor health and sanitation conditions that existed in West Virginia at the time, which were solely accountable for the high mortality rate among children. She was a skilled orator and worked to create a banded workforce among mothers to take on social issues. She called these clubs The Mothers Day Work Clubs. It was her lifelong wish that someone commemorate a special day devoted to and honoring mothers.

The state by state campaign launched by her daughter Anna after her death in 1905 took years and all of her personal fortune to complete. Filled with the same fiery determination, Anna took on the Herculean task of making her mother's wish come true.

Never a mother herself, Anna systematically created a grassroots movement to have the second Sunday of the month denoted Mother's Day by creating committees and engaging powerful political allies, philanthropists, and influential friends. One by one, states adopted the holiday, and by 1914, her efforts were successful, and Mother's Day became an official national holiday.

To explain the intent of the day, Anna Jarvis wrote:

> This day is intended that we may make new resolutions for a more active thought to our dear mothers…To revive the dormant filial love and gratitude we owe to those who gave us birth. To be a home tie for the absent. To obliterate family estrangement. To make us better children by getting us closer to the hearts of our good mothers. To brighten the lives of good mothers. To have them know we appreciate them, though we do not show it as often as we ought…Mothers Day is to remind us of our duty before it is too late.

Anna's crusade to create a day to memorialize her mother and commemorate all mothers began and ended with her undying love and appreciation for her own mother, a woman who made such a deep impression on her person that she spent all her inheritance, time and much of her life devoted to making her dream a reality.

Do not think that love, in order to be genuine, has to be extraordinary. What we need is to love without getting tired.

Mother Teresa, Missionary

Oddly, one of the greatest mothers who actually assumed that moniker as part of her name, never actually gave birth. Rather, she was a mother to humanity and all mankind. Mother Teresa was born Agnes Gonxha Bojaxhiu in 1910 in Yugoslavia. She became a woman of the cloth when she joined the Sisters of Loreto in 1928.

As her quote suggests, love doesn't have to be extraordinary in order to be genuine and miraculous. It just had to be tireless. And that is the true key and sterling characteristic of motherly love. It's undying and selfless.

It was her internal motivator, this unbridled capacity to love and keep loving in the face of dire circumstances which set her apart. She dedicated the majority of her life to helping the poorest of the poor in India, thus gaining her the name "Saint of the Gutters." She founded an order of nuns called the Missionaries of Charity in Calcutta, India, dedicated to serving the poor, with over 3,000 throughout 100 countries worldwide. She won the Nobel Peace Prize in 1979. Mother Teresa died in 1997 at the age of 86.

What she has left behind, however, has been a testimony to the life she lived. Mother Teresa encompasses what we honor most as maternal qualities: selflessness, nurturing, compassion, unconditional love, and saintliness. Her legacy shows what the power of one tiny woman with an enormous heart and ironclad determination, dedication, and love for humanity can do. She is a sterling example of the best of motherhood.

A Legacy
of Love

My mother was the making of me.
She was so true and so sure of me,
I felt that I had someone to live for;
someone I must not disappoint.
The memory of my mother will
always be a blessing to me.

Thomas A. Edison, Inventor

There is a saintliness about motherhood. Many famous historical figures often reference their own mothers in such esteem, such as Thomas Edison's clear devotion to his mother, viewing them as women of unparalleled goodness, love, dedication, and support. Leaders of nations and distinguished thinkers all carry a devotion to their mothers that is inspiring.

My mother was the most beautiful woman I ever saw. All I am I owe to my mother. I attribute all my success in life to the moral, intellectual and physical education I received from her.

George Washington, U.S. President

Philosophers, poets, and great writers over time have striven to capture the essence of this complex and profound relationship with their mothers, in such a way as to paint it—divine.

The heart of a mother is a deep abyss at the bottom of which you will always find forgiveness.

Honoré de Balzac, Writer

It is an honor to be counted in those ranks, and every mother's dream to be described as such. While the famous and notable have had much to say about the relationship between a child and mother, this bond in all its commonalities continues to be unique and indescribable.

How you are remembered by your children is what matters most. And what better gauge of that is there than how your children live their lives and how they love? You may not be here to know about it or enjoy it. Hopefully, you will be long gone to dust when your children gray and mature. But your children will come to their places in adulthood eventually. Perhaps then, they will fully appreciate the gift that you have given them. Insight might bless them and they will see, if only at a glimpse, the precious gift of that maternal love, in all its nuances.

Your children know how it feels to be loved by you. Not because you told them, but because they lived that love. In every time you sat up late at night, holding onto your sanity, barely breathing from worry. In every brush of your hand to fix an errant stray hair. In every time you didn't grimace when they pushed that hand away. A mother's love is a warm embrace when tears come, a reverent silence when one is needed, a strict word when a boundary is pushed, and a wave goodbye when all you want to do is hold your children forever. A mother's kiss can be a ham sandwich with chips on a glass plate, a ride to the movies in a rainstorm, or the gesture of handing them the keys to your car when they really need it. Or perhaps it's a silent prayer said in the middle of the night, thanking the stars for these wondrous people who have made you multi-dimensional and ultimately enriched your life.

The legacy of motherhood is so profound. It is hard to wrap your arms around it. Your love, a mother's love, has the ability to sustain you because it is indeed a legacy. The impact made on your children will be felt for generations to come. As time passes and the cycle of life continues, your children and your children's children will pass on what you have given today. The impact of maternal love is far-reaching.

Never forget when times get tough, or sad or confusing, that doing the best you can, can and will have its rewards. Many of those rewards are evident in the moment. Some take time to gestate. Other rewards you will never know but they will be imprinted on the universe and felt for generations to come. There is a timelessness to your maternal love that will leave a hand print on those that you don't even know, and may never know. Nothing else in the world can claim that privilege.

They say that our mothers live on through us. As such, we will live on through our children and so it goes on and on, lifetime after lifetime. It is the infinite nature of unconditional, motherly love and the importance of each and every mother. And as it cycles through decades of time and generations of children, it refines itself, growing broader and better with each turn. You have a large part in how that refinement process continues. Waste nary a moment in wondering about that. Who you are to your children is poignantly important to them and the cycle of life.

They are flesh of your flesh, born of you not only physically, but emotionally and spiritually. The connection is strong not so much because of the biological ties but because of who you are in their lives and growth. Never question it, never worry about, for it just is. And the best of you is what they will carry forth into their own lives.

Whether you are fully aware of it or not, your hand will touch each and every generation that bears your name. You will be called granny or great-grandmother if you are lucky. But be secure in the fact that in generations to come, while you the person might not be remembered, your love will live on. And that is your legacy as a mother.

The Art of Mothering: *Words and Wisdom*

A Mother's Great Love

✳ ✳ ✳

Motherhood: All love begins and ends there.

Robert Browning, Poet

A man loves his sweetheart the most; his wife the best; and his mother the longest.

Irish Proverb

The mother loves her child most divinely, not when she surrounds him with comfort and anticipates his wants, but when she resolutely holds him to the highest standards and is content with nothing less than his best.

Hamilton Wright Mabie, Writer

Motherly love is not much use if it expresses itself only as a warm gush of emotion, delicately tinged with pink. It must also be strong, guiding and unselfish. The sweetly sung lullaby; the cool hand on the fevered brow, the Mother's Day smiles and flowers are only a small part of the picture. True mothers have to be made of steel to withstand the difficulties that are sure to beset their children.

Rachel Billington, Writer

MOTHERING: THE ULTIMATE JOB

✳ ✳ ✳

I looked on child-rearing not only as a work of love and
duty but as a profession that was fully as interesting and
challenging as any honorable profession in the world
and one that demanded the best that I could bring it.

Rose Kennedy, Socialite

*By and large, mothers and housewives are the
only workers who do not have regular time off.
They are the great vacationless class.*

Anne Morrow Lindbergh, Aviator

Nobody knows of the work it makes
To keep the home together.
Nobody knows of the steps it takes,
Nobody knows—but Mother.

Anonymous

At work, you think of the children
you have left at home. At home, you think
of the work you've left unfinished.
Such a struggle is unleashed within yourself.
Your heart is rent.

Golda Meir, Prime Minister of Israel

If you bungle raising your children,

I don't think whatever else you do well

matters very much.

Jacqueline Kennedy Onassis, U.S. First Lady

The best way to keep children home
is to make the home atmosphere pleasant
and let the air out of the tires.

Dorothy Parker, Writer

Women do not have to sacrifice personhood if they are mothers. They do not have to sacrifice motherhood in order to be persons. Liberation was meant to expand women's opportunities, not to limit them. The self-esteem that has been found in new pursuits can also be found in mothering.

Elaine Heffner, Psychiatrist

Those who say they "sleep like a baby" haven't got one.

A new mother

Never being number one in your list of priorities and not minding at all.

Jasmine Guinness, Fashion Model

To be a mother is a woman's greatest vocation in life. She is a partner with God. No being has a position of such power and influence. She holds in her hands the destiny of nations, for to her comes the responsibility and opportunity of molding the nation's citizens.

Spencer W. Kimball, Church Leader

There is no point at which you can say, "Well, I'm successful now. I might as well take a nap."

Carrie Fisher, Actor

A vacation frequently means that the family goes away for a rest, accompanied by mother, who sees that the others get it.

Marcelene Cox, Writer

There never was a child so lovely but his mother was glad to get him asleep.

Ralph Waldo Emerson, Writer

My mother had a great deal of trouble with me, but I think she enjoyed it.

Mark Twain, Writer

The story of a mother's life:
Trapped between a scream and a hug.

Cathy Guisewite, Cartoonist

THE MOTHER-CHILD BOND

✳ ✳ ✳

I saw pure love when my son looked at me,
and I knew that I had to make a good life
for the two of us.

Suzanne Somers, Actor

The mother-child relationship is
paradoxical and, in a sense, tragic.
It requires the most intense love on the
mother's side, yet this very love must
help the child grow away from the mother
and to become fully independent.

Erich Fromm, Psychoanalyst

A mother is not a person to
lean on, but a person to make
leaning unnecessary.

Dorothy Canfield Fisher, Writer

Children make you want to start life over.

Muhammad Ali, Professional Boxer

It will be gone before you know it. The fingerprints on the wall appear higher and higher. Then suddenly they disappear.

Dorothy Evslin, Writer

One generation plants the trees; another gets the shade.

Chinese Proverb

Then someone placed her in my arms. She looked up at me. The crying stopped. Her eyes melted through me, forging a connection in me with their soft heat.

Shirley MacLaine, Actor

Parents were invented to make children happy by giving them something to ignore.

Ogden Nash, Poet

There is nothing more thrilling in this world, I think, than having a child that is yours, and yet is mysteriously a stranger.

Agatha Christie, Writer

Motherhood cannot finally be delegated.
Breast-feeding may succumb to the bottle;
cuddling, fondling, and pediatric visits may
also be done by fathers…but when a child
needs a mother to talk to, nobody else but
a mother will do.

Erica Jong, Writer

A sweater is a garment worn by a child
when the mother feels chill.

Barbara Johnson, Literary Critic

When you are a mother, you are never really alone in your thoughts. You are connected to your child and to all those who touch your lives. A mother always has to think twice: Once of herself and once for her child.

Sophia Loren, Actor

Making the decision to have a child—it's momentous. It is to decide forever to have your heart go walking around outside your body.

Elizabeth Stone, Writer

The Village Voice

January 15, 1985

CHILDREN ARE TREASURES

❈ ❈ ❈

Children are the anchors that hold a mother to life.

Sophocles, Dramatist

When I approach a child, he inspires in me two sentiments;
tenderness for what he is, and respect for what he may become.

Louis Pasteur, Biologist

Life's aspirations come in the guise of children.

Rabindranath Tagore, Writer

Children need your presence
more than your presents.

Jesse Jackson, Politician

People always talked about a mother's uncanny
ability to read her children, but that was nothing
compared to how children could read their mothers.

Anne Tyler, Writer

Never lend your car to anyone to whom
you have given birth.

Erma Bombeck, Writer

PRAISE FOR MOTHERS

✳ ✳ ✳

*All that I am and I ever hope to be
I owe to my angel mother.*

Abraham Lincoln, U.S. President

Of all the rights of women,
the greatest is to be a mother.

Lin Yutang, Writer

*I think my life began with waking up
and loving my mother's face.*

George Eliot, Writer

A mother is the truest friend we have, when trials, heavy and sudden, fall upon us; when adversity takes the place of prosperity; when friends who rejoice with us in our sunshine, desert us when troubles thicken around us, still will she cling to us, and endeavor by her kind precepts and counsels to dissipate the clouds of darkness, and cause peace to return to our hearts.

Washington Irving, Writer

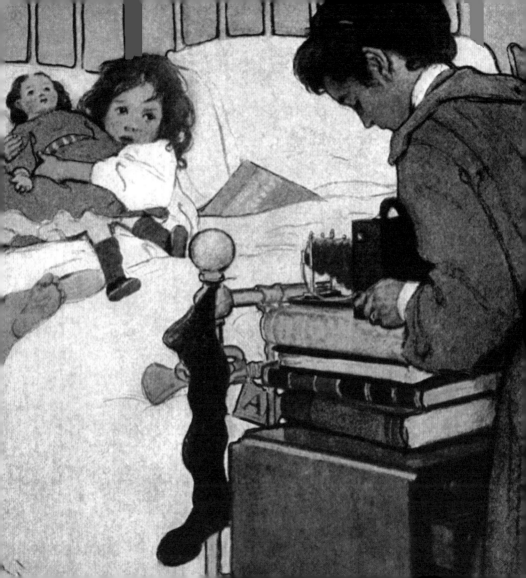

There never was a woman like her. She was gentle as a dove and brave as a lioness. The memory of my mother and her teachings were, after all, the only capital I had to start life with, and on that capital I have made my way.

Andrew Jackson, U.S. President

It seems to me that my mother was the most splendid woman I ever knew. I have met a lot of people knocking around the world since, but I have never met a more thoroughly refined woman than my mother. If I have amounted to anything, it will be due to her.

Charlie Chaplin, Actor

I love being a mother…I am more aware. I feel things on a deeper level. I have a kind of understanding about my body, about being a woman.

Shelley Long, Actor

Everybody knows that a good mother gives her children a feeling of trust and stability. She is their earth. She is the one they can count on for the things that matter most of all…There is no substitute for her. Somehow even her clothes feel different to her children's hands from anybody else's clothes. Only to touch her skirt or her sleeve makes a troubled child feel better.

Katharine Butler Hathaway, Writer

A mother is a person who seeing there are only four pieces of pie for five people, promptly announces she never did care for pie.

Tenneva Jordan, Writer

She is my first, great love. She was a wonderful, rare woman—you do not know; as strong, and steadfast, and generous as the sun. She could be as swift as a white whiplash, and as kind and gentle as warm rain, and as steadfast as the irreducible earth beneath us.

D. H. Lawrence, Writer

Mother: the most beautiful word
on the lips of mankind.

Kahlil Gibran, Writer

There was never a great man who had not
a great mother.

Olive Schreiner, Writer

It is not that I half knew my mother. I knew half of
her: the lower half—her lap, legs, feet, her hands
and wrists as she bent forward.

Flann O'Brien, Writer

Fifty-four years of love and tenderness and crossness and devotion and unswerving loyalty. Without her I could have achieved a quarter of what I have achieved, not only in terms of success and career, but in terms of personal happiness. She has never stood between me and my life, never tried to hold me too tightly, always let me go free.

Noël Coward, Dramatist

The doctors told me that I would never walk, but my mother told me I would, so I believed my mother.

Wilma Rudolph, Athlete

As a mother, my job is to take care

of the possible and trust God

with the impossible.

Ruth Bell Graham, Writer

Mothers Day is in honor of the

best Mother who ever lived—

the Mother of your heart.

Anna Jarvis, Founder of Mother's Day

A MOTHER'S LEGACY

✳ ✳ ✳

She tried in every way to understand me, and she succeeded. It was this deep, loving understanding as long as she lived that more than anything else helped and sustained me on my way to success.

Mae West, Actor

There is so much to teach,
and the time goes so fast.

Erma Bombeck, Writer

Motherhood is the greatest potential influence in human society. Her caress first awakens in the child a sense of security; her kiss the first realization of affection; her sympathy and tenderness, the first assurance that there is love in the world. Thus in infancy and childhood she implants ever-directing and restraining influences that remain through life.

David O. McKay, Church Leader

It is not what you do for your children but what you have taught them to do for themselves that will make them successful human beings.

Ann Landers, Writer

Each day of our lives we make deposits in the memory banks of our children.

Charles R. Swindoll, Pastor

My mother wanted me to be her wings, to fly as she never quite had the courage to do. I love her for that. I love the fact that she wanted to give birth to her own wings.

Erica Jong, Writer

The mother is the most precious possession of the nation, so precious that society advances its highest well-being when it protects the functions of the mother.

Ellen Key, Writer

And Always
Remember...

When the tough times come, as they often will, and the waters seem unnavigable and strange, you can take comfort in several things:

❋ You are never alone. Every mother who is worth her salt has navigated these waters, too. While they are unfamiliar to you, they are universally understood by all mothers through the ages. Draw from their experiences and fuel your life from their expertise. Find comfort in those who have gone before.

❋ You can do this. Remember back when you brought this baby home, scared to death that you wouldn't make it through the night without doing something very wrong. It's a learn-as-you-go life lesson, and one that builds upon itself.

Love yourself, love your child, and take joy in each and every moment.

About Cider Mill Press Book Publishers

Good ideas ripen with time. From seed to harvest, Cider Mill Press strives to bring fine reading, information, and entertainment together between the covers of its creatively crafted books. Our Cider Mill bears fruit twice a year, publishing a new crop of titles each spring and fall.

CIDER MILL PRESS

BOOK PUBLISHERS

*Where Good Books are
Ready for Press*

Visit us on the web at
www.cidermillpress.com
or write to us at
12 Port Farm Road
Kennebunkport, Maine 04046